ACCOUNTABILITY

"Let us hear the conclusion of the whole matter: Fear God, and keep His commandments: for this is the whole duty of man. For God shall bring every work into judgment, with every secret thing, whether it be good, or whether it be evil."

—Ecclesiastes 12:13,14
The Holy Bible

"The Instructions You Follow Determine The Future You Create."
-MIKE MURDOCK

2

ANGER

"He that is slow to anger is better than the mighty; and he that ruleth his spirit than he that taketh a city."

–Proverbs 16:32
The Holy Bible

"Anger Is Merely Passion
Requiring Appropriate Focus ."
-MIKE MURDOCK

3

ASSIGNMENT

"Before I formed thee in the belly I knew thee; and before thou camest forth out of the womb I sanctified thee, and I ordained thee a prophet unto the nations."

–Jeremiah 1:5
The Holy Bible

"Those Who Unlock Your Passion Are Those To Whom You Have Been Assigned."

-MIKE MURDOCK

4

BUSINESS

"Seest thou a man diligent in his business? he shall stand before kings; he shall not stand before mean men."

–Proverbs 22:29
The Holy Bible

"The Problems You Solve Determine The Rewards You Receive."
-MIKE MURDOCK

5

CHILDREN

"Lo, children are an heritage of the Lord: and the fruit of the womb is his reward. As arrows are in the hand of a mighty man; so are children of the youth. Happy is the man that hath his quiver full of them: they shall not be ashamed, but they shall speak with the enemies in the gate."

–Psalm 127:3-5
The Holy Bible

*"The Proof Of Love
Is the Desire To Protect."*
-MIKE MURDOCK

6

CHURCH

"One thing have I desired of the Lord, that will I seek after; that I may dwell in the house of the Lord all the days of my life, to behold the beauty of the Lord, and to enquire in His temple, For in the time of trouble He shall hide me in His pavilion: in the secret of His tabernacle shall He hide me; He shall set me up upon a rock."

–Psalm 27:4,5
The Holy Bible

"Where You Are Determines What Grows Within You."
-MIKE MURDOCK

7

CRISIS

"When thou passest through the waters, I will be with thee; and through the rivers, they shall not overflow thee: when thou walkest through the fire, thou shalt not be burned; neither shall the flame kindle upon thee."

–Isaiah 43:2
The Holy Bible

"Crisis Always Occurs At The Curve Of Change."
-MIKE MURDOCK

8

CRITICAL ATTITUDE

"Death and life are in the power of the tongue: and they that love it shall eat the fruit thereof."

–Proverbs 18:21
The Holy Bible

"You Cannot Improve What You Destroy."
-MIKE MURDOCK

9

DEBT

"The Lord shall open unto thee His good treasure, the heaven to give the rain unto thy land in His season, and to bless all the work of thine hand: and thou shalt lend unto many nations, and thou shalt not borrow."

–Deuteronomy 28:12
The Holy Bible

"The Proof Of Maturity Is The Ability To Delay Gratification."
-MIKE MURDOCK

10

DISCIPLINE OF CHILDREN

"Correct thy son, and he shall give thee rest; yea, he shall give delight unto thy soul."

–Proverbs 29:17
The Holy Bible

"Anything Permitted Will Increase."
-MIKE MURDOCK

11

FINANCES

"Praise ye the Lord. Blessed is the man that feareth the Lord, that delighteth greatly in His commandments. Wealth and riches shall be in his house: and his righteousness endureth for ever."

–Psalm 112:1,3
The Holy Bible

"Prosperity Is Having Enough Of God's Provision To Complete His Instructions For Your Life."

-MIKE MURDOCK

12

FOCUS

"Only be thou strong and very courageous, that thou mayest observe to do according to all the law, which Moses my servant commanded thee: turn not from it to the right hand or to the left, that thou mayest prosper whithersoever thou goest. This book of the law shall not depart out of thy mouth; but thou shalt meditate therein day and night, that thou mayest observe to do according to all that is written therein: for then thou shalt make thy way prosperous, and then thou shalt have good success." –Joshua 1:7,8

The Holy Bible

"The Only Reason Men Fail Is Broken Focus."

-MIKE MURDOCK

13

FRIENDSHIP

"He that walketh with wise men shall be wise: but a companion of fools shall be destroyed."

–Proverbs 13:20
The Holy Bible

"Someone You Are Trusting Is Trusting Someone Else You Would Not."

-MIKE MURDOCK

14

JOB

"Whatsoever thy hand findeth to do, do it with thy might."

–Ecclesiastes 9:10a
The Holy Bible

"You Can Only Be Promoted By The Person Whose Instructions You Have Followed."
-MIKE MURDOCK

15

LEADERSHIP

"...as for me and my house, we will serve the Lord."

–Joshua 24:15
The Holy Bible

*"You Have No Right To Anything
You Have Not Pursued."*

-MIKE MURDOCK

16

LOVE

"And now abideth faith, hope, charity, these three; but the greatest of these is charity."

– 1 Corinthians 13:13
The Holy Bible

"The Proof Of Love
Is The Investment Of Time."
-MIKE MURDOCK

17

MARRIAGE

"Husbands, love your wives, even as Christ also loved the church, and gave Himself for it; So ought men to love their wives as their own bodies. He that loveth his wife loveth himself. For no man ever yet hated his own flesh; but nourisheth and cherisheth it, even as the Lord the church."

–Ephesians 5:25,28,29
The Holy Bible

"The Proof Of Love
Is The Willingiess To Protect."
-MIKE MURDOCK

18

MENTORSHIP

"And these words, which I command thee this day, shall be in thine heart: And thou shalt teach them diligently unto thy children, and shalt talk of them when thou sittest in thine house, and when thou walkest by the way, and when thou liest down, and when thou risest up."

–Deuteronomy 6:6,7
The Holy Bible

"You Will Only Remember What You Teach."

-MIKE MURDOCK

19

OVERCOMING

"Wherefore take unto you the whole armour of God, that ye may be able to withstand in the evil day, and having done all, to stand"

- Ephesians 6:13
The Holy Bible

"The Size Of Your Enemy Determines The Size Of Your Reward."

-MIKE MURDOCK

20

PATIENCE

"And, ye fathers, provoke not your children to wrath: but bring them up in the nurture and admonition of the Lord."

–Ephesians 6:4
The Holy Bible

"What You Love Will Eventually Reward You."
-MIKE MURDOCK

21

PRAYER

"If ye abide in Me, and My words abide in you, ye shall ask what ye will, and it shall be done unto you."

-John 15:7
The Holy Bible

"The Proof Of Humility Is The Willingness To Reach."

-MIKE MURDOCK

22

PRESENCE OF GOD

"Thou wilt shew me the path of life: in Thy presence is fulness of joy; at Thy right hand there are pleasures for evermore." –Psalm 16:11
The Holy Bible

"The Presence Of God Is The Only Place Your Weakness Can Die."
-MIKE MURDOCK

23

PROBLEM SOLVING

"Knowing that whatsoever good thing any man doeth, the same shall he receive of the Lord, whether he be bond or free." –Ephesians 6:8
The Holy Bible

"The Problems You Solve Determine The Rewards You Receive."
-MIKE MURDOCK

24

RECOVERY

"And I will restore to you the years that the locust hath eaten, the cankerworm, and the caterpiller, and the palmerworm, my great army which I sent among you."

–Joel 2:25
The Holy Bible

*"What Men Takes Away—
God Will Restore."*
-MIKE MURDOCK

25

STRIFE

"And the servant of the Lord must not strive; but be gentle unto all men, apt to teach, patient."

-2 Timothy 2:24
The Holy Bible

"Pain Is The Proof Of Disorder."
-MIKE MURDOCK

26

STRESS

"I can do all things through Christ which strengtheneth me."

-Philippians 4:13
The Holy Bible

"Losers Focus On What They Are Going Through—Champions Focus On What They Are Going To."

-MIKE MURDOCK

27

TEMPTATION

"There hath no temptation taken you but such as is common to man: but God is faithful, Who will not suffer you to be tempted above that ye are able; but will with the temptation also make a way to escape, that ye may be able to bear it."

– 1 Corinthians 10:13
The Holy Bible

"Champions Walk Away From Something They Desire To Protect Something Else They Love."
-MIKE MURDOCK

28

THE SECRET PLACE

"He that dwelleth in The Secret Place of the most High shall abide under the shadow of the Almighty."

–Psalm 91:1
The Holy Bible

"The Atmosphere You Permit Determines The Person You Become."
-MIKE MURDOCK

29

TITHING

"Bring ye all the tithes into the storehouse, that there may be meat in Mine house, and prove me now herewith, saith the Lord of hosts, if I will not open you the windows of heaven, and pour you out a blessing, that there shall not be room enough to receive it."

–Malachi 3:10
The Holy Bible

"If You Keep Something God Did Not Give You, He Will Take Back Something He Gave You."

-MIKE MURDOCK

30

WISDOM

"Wisdom is the principal thing; therefore get wisdom: and with all thy getting get understanding."

–Proverbs 4:7
The Holy Bible

"Every Problem Is Simply A Wisdom Problem."
-MIKE MURDOCK

31

WORD OF GOD

"Thou through Thy commandments hast made me wiser than mine enemies: for they are ever with me."

–Psalm 119:98
The Holy Bible

"What You Keep Hearing You Eventually Believe."
-MIKE MURDOCK

DECISION

Will You Accept Jesus As Your Personal Savior Today?

The Bible says, "That if thou shalt confess with thy mouth the Lord Jesus, and shalt believe in thine heart that God hath raised Him from the dead, thou shalt be saved" (Romans 10:9).

Pray this prayer from your heart today! *"Dear Jesus, I believe that You died for me and rose again on the third day. I confess I am a sinner...I need Your love and forgiveness...Come into my heart. Forgive my sins. I receive Your eternal life. Confirm Your love by giving me peace, joy and supernatural love for others. Amen."*

☐ Yes, Mike! I made a decision to accept Christ as my personal Savior today. Please send me my free gift of your book *"31 Keys to a New Beginning"* to help me with my new life in Christ. *(B-48)*

NAME _____

ADDRESS _____

CITY _____ STATE _____ ZIP _____

PHONE ( ) _____ EMAIL _____

Mail To: **The Wisdom Center**   *(B-180)*
P.O. Box 99 · Denton, TX 76202
1-888-WISDOM-1 (1-888-947-3661)
Website: www.thewisdomcenter.tv

Unless otherwise indicated, all Scripture quotations are taken from the King James Version of the Bible.
31 Scriptures Every Father Should Memorize · ISBN 1-56394-274-7-B-180
Copyright © 2003 by **MIKE MURDOCK**
All publishing rights belong exclusively to Wisdom International
Published by The Wisdom Center · P.O. Box 99 · Denton, Texas 76202
1-888-WISDOM-1 (1-888-947-3661) · Website: www.thewisdomcenter.tv
Printed in the United States of America. All rights reserved under International Copyright Law. Contents and/or cover may not be reproduced in whole or in part in any form without the expressed written consent of the publisher.   05030100K

BUSINESS REPLY MAIL
FIRST CLASS   PERMIT NO. 4459   DENTON, TEXAS

POSTAGE WILL BE PAID BY ADDRESSEE

THE
WISDOM
CENTER

MIKE MURDOCK

P.O. BOX 99
Denton, TX 76202-9951

Your Search Is Over.

Order from our website: www.thewisdomcenter.tv

The Holy Spirit, The Assignment, and The Seed.
These three vital topics deserve your Total Focus:
The Holy Spirit Is The *Source* Of Your Life.
The Assignment Is The *Reason* For Your Life.
The Seed Is The *Provision* For Your Life.

B-180

Wisdom Is The Principal Thing
$10
B-101
The Wisdom Center

THE 3 MOST IMPORTANT THINGS IN YOUR LIFE

MIKE MURDOCK
Over 3 Million Mike Murdock Books In Print

Order Today!
1-888-WISDOM-1
(1-888-947-3661)

The Wisdom Center
P.O. Box 99
Denton, Texas 76202
www.thewisdomcenter.tv

THE WISDOM CENTER

1-888-WISDOM-1 (1-888-947-3661)

PRODUCT NUMBER	PRODUCT DESCRIPTION	QTY	PRICE	TOTAL
				1
				2
				3
				4
				5
				6

		SubTotal	7
	Canada ADD 20%		8
	S/H Add 10%		9
		TOTAL $	10
My Seed Offering $			11

Bookstore Discounts
(assorted titles!)

QTY.	DISCOUNT
1-9	Retail
10-499	40%
500-1999	50%
2000-4999	60%
5000 & Up	Contact Office

Name

Address

City ___ State ___ Zip

Phone ___ Email

Method of Payment
☐ Cash   ☐ Check   ☐ Visa   ☐ MC   ☐ Amex   ☐ Discover

Card#

Birthday MO / DAY   Expiration Date

Total Enclosed $ ___ Signature

(Sorry No C.O.D.'s)

B-180

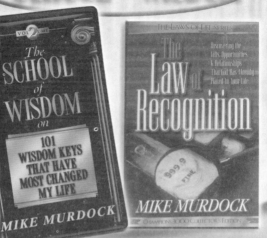
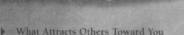

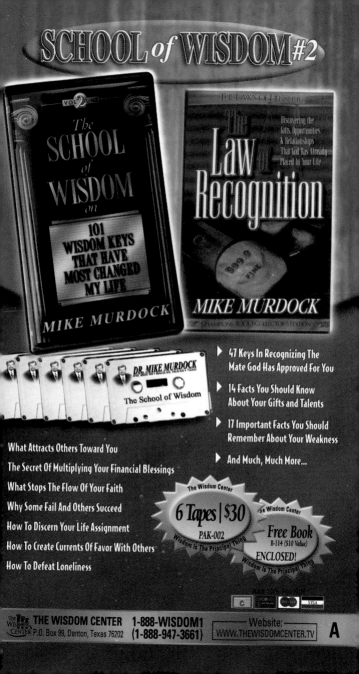

Financial Success.

8 Scriptural Reasons You Should
Pursue Financial Prosperity

The Secret Prayer Key You Need When
Making A Financial Request To God

The Weapon Of Expectation And The
5 Miracles It Unlocks

How To Discern Those Who Qualify
To Receive Your Financial Assistance

How To Predict The Miracle Moment
God Will Schedule Your Financial
Breakthrough

Habits Of Uncommon Achievers

The Greatest Success Law I Ever
Discovered

▸ How To Discern Your Place
Of Assignment, The Only
Place Financial Provision Is
Guaranteed

▸ 3 Secret Keys In Solving
Problems For Others

The Wisdom Center

Video Pak
AMVIDEO | $30
Buy 1 Get 1 Free
(A $60 Value!)
Wisdom Is The Principal Thing

Add 10% For S/H

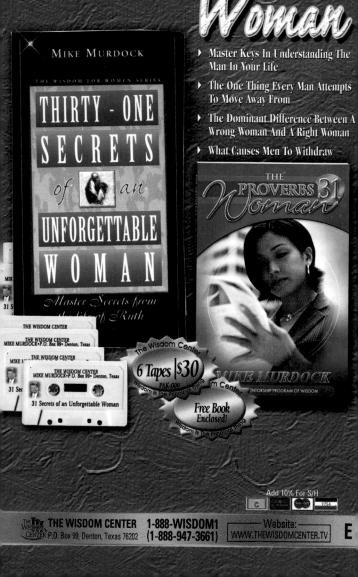